THE SELLING PLAN

HOW TO GET NEW CUSTOMERS, MAKE MORE MONEY AND SELL LIKE CRAZY

EMMA JONES

THE SELLING PLAN

HOW TO GET NEW CUSTOMERS, MAKE MORE MONEY AND SELL LIKE CRAZY

By

EMMA JONES

GRAB MY FREE COURSE

Do you need more leads for your business?

Need more clients?

Would you like to know how to ATTRACT leads to you online, using social media, without having to chase or bug family and friends?

Get Access To My Free Course Here

Also by Emma Jones

Instagram Influencer: How To Use Instagram For Business, Sales, Marketing & Growth

Get Your Copy Now:

TABLE OF CONTENTS

CHAPTER 1 - IMAGINE THIS…

What if every time you spoke to a prospect you had a proven step by step process to follow.

A process that is almost guaranteed to get your prospect to say YES to taking a look at what it is you have to offer, joining your opportunity or buying your product.

And it doesn't matter what you're selling either.

The Selling Plan stays the same, no matter whether you're selling a $50 skincare cream or a $30,000 coaching program.

What would it be like, instead of being nervous and trying to convince your prospect, that your prospect actually convinced and closed themselves?

Sound too good to be true? I know exactly how you feel.
I felt the same way until I was taught a process that I'm going to share with you in this book…

It's a process called, 'The Selling Plan' and it's used through a series of powerful questions with your prospects that lead to closing the sale.

This process has worked so well for me, that in the time I have been using this process I have been able to close sales worth $43,461 in just 90 days.

This process also allowed me to close $150k of sales in a single weekend. (I was selling higher ticket offers at the weekend event, which shows that this process works no matter what the price point is).

With the Selling Plan Formula we walk the prospect through a series of questions that will allow your prospect to *convince themselves* that they need your product or service.

The questions and conversations are completely authentic.

There is no trickery involved here, and nor should there ever be in sales.

It's about allowing your prospect to discover their desire and needs and you simply *offer your product or service as the solution.*

What's also really important with the Selling Plan Formula is that we also weed out the time wasters and tyre kickers early on, *(this is not something you do at the end, you do it at the start of your conversations).*

Imagine that you ONLY speak to qualified prospects and you never have to waste time with people who were never really going to be interested in the first place.

This is a powerful part of the process that will allow you to truly make the most of your time.

Once your prospect has taken a look at your product/service or opportunity we then need to close the prospect, again using powerful questions and handling objections.

If you have followed the process step by step you will have all the information you need to help close your prospect.

This is the beauty of having a process to follow.

You can never go wrong speaking to your prospect.

You will always know what to do next.

You won't ever come away from your conversation thinking, 'I totally winged that', or have that feeling of the conversation just went horribly wrong.

And be honest, how many times have you spoken with a client or a prospect and thought that way? That you 'winged' it?

What I just gave you, is an overview of the exact process I follow, every time I close a sale, whether it's $100, $3000 or $30,000.

And I'm about to reveal it to you, step by step, in this book so let's dive in.

In this book I'll show you how you can;

- Get more people to say YES to taking a look at your product or opportunity

- Gather important information about your prospect that will help you to close the sale.
- Have your prospect convince themselves that this is a right fit for them
- Make sure you spend your precious time only speaking to qualified prospects by weeding out time-wasters early on.
- Cover the 'up-front contract' formula, so you can have your prospects agreeing to you making them an offer (game-changer)
- Be set up with the powerful questions process. So you know what to ask, and when, and will never be 'winging' a conversation again.

I will also show you how to close the sale and handle objections like a pro so you can;

- Sell more of your products and have more people join your opportunity.
- Have a process to follow and always know what you need to do next to get people closer to saying yes

- Overcome objections like a pro, by asking powerful questions.

CHAPTER 2 - EMMA'S STORY

I have always had a sales background.

Even in my early days, just when I left school, I went straight into a career within sales and marketing selling credit cards with a big firm in the UK.

Sales has always been in my blood, in one way or another.

Fast forward to 2012 and I found myself within the home based business industry. Specifically Network Marketing.

When I first joined the Network Marketing industry, I used to talk to hundreds of prospects to try and close sales.

Sometimes they were my own prospects, a lot of the time they were 3 way calls for my team and downline.

Now don't get me wrong, I closed a lot of people in these conversations, but I also had a lot of people who said *no*.

I wasted a *lot* of time chasing people, the wrong people, being ignored and faced a lot of rejection.

The biggest thing about these conversations was this.

Every single time *I was winging it.* I had no process, no strategy and quite frankly, I was just hoping that our conversation would result in someone saying yes.

How many times have you found yourself in that situation?

When someone joined I had no way of being able to tell what I did right in order to close the sale.

The same as when someone didn't join, I had no way of being able to tell what I did wrong.

That was until I discovered the 'Selling Plan' process.

I immersed myself in this training and was lucky enough to be coached and trained by some of the best in the industry

I was also lucky enough to be hired as a business consultation coach for a big reputable company in the home based business industry where I've coached *thousands* and applied this process over and over again.

I've had a lot of practice!

This process alone allowed me to close $150,000 worth of sales in one single weekend.

When I say a single weekend really it was in less than 12 hours.

The Selling Plan process works.

One of the best parts about it is, you never have to 'wing' a single sales conversation again.

Full disclaimer here, my results aren't typical, and I can't guarantee that you'll get the same results as I have.

But what I can say is this, with the Selling Plan process, you will always have a strategy that you can follow, step-by-step, every time you speak to a prospect that is much more likely to have your prospects saying *YES.*

Sound good?

Let's dive in.

CHAPTER 3 - THE FIRST MEETING WITH YOUR PROSPECT

Everything I'm about to teach you works, no matter what the medium is.

Obviously there's you; the person selling whatever product or service it is you're selling.

And there's your prospect, client, whatever language you'd like to use here. It doesn't matter.

This is the person who is going to be 'buying'.

Now, it's also important to note too, that even though I'm saying buying, this could also mean joining.

Point being, you're looking to 'close' this prospect on whatever deal it is you're offering.

The process works the same every time.

However, in my opinion the **best** way to close a prospect is by actually speaking to them.

We'll cover more reasons about this further on.

There are many factors that increase your chances of closing a sale when you physically speak with someone.

Now, this doesn't have to be face to face, or even over the phone.

It also doesn't have to include your voice (however this really helps and again will increase your conversions).

But you'd be surprised at the amount of people that will try to shy away from this.

They'll try to get away with just a presentation, or messages.

However, when you actually talk with someone, you are giving yourself a much higher chance of closing the sale.

Doesn't matter if this is over the phone, using some sort of video chat (where I've had my most success) or again, face to face.

The medium does not matter.

The process does.

The Intention of that first conversation

Typically, when a prospect speaks to you for the first time, they are looking for more information.

What most people do in this situation is they give them the information.

This is where most people go wrong.

One of the secrets to the Selling Plan, is not giving the prospect what they want straight off the bat.

Your intention on that first conversation is to actually set the right intention from the start, not to give all the goods away.

You are letting them know right out of the gate that you are in control of this conversation.

This is critical.

If you are in control of the conversation, you are much more likely to close the sale.

Position your first conversation as a consultation

When setting up the first conversation with your prospect, position it as a consultation.

This is what positioning that conversation as a consultation does;

1. It instantly says to your prospect that you're going to be asking questions. Because typically that is what a consultation is. (And as you'll discover throughout this book, questions are the key to becoming a master closer)
2. It positions you as the expert. In your prospects mind they instantly see you as an expert, because you're not just saying, " Ok, let's have a chat,"

a consultation sounds like you actually have a process.

3. It sounds, and is much more professional. Let's face it, wouldn't you rather buy something, or join someone who positions themselves as an expert? Clearly someone who is professional and knows what they're doing? This is just one way you set yourself apart from your competition. You get serious about what you're doing.

4. It allows you to be in control of the sale from the start (even though with this process we're going to make the prospect think they're in charge, but they're not. You are in charge every step of the way, and need to be if you want to close the sale)

5. Your prospect will feel more comfortable knowing you're in control. They're happy for you to be steering this conversation!

CHAPTER 4 - WHERE MOST PEOPLE GO WRONG

In my years of selling and experience coaching thousands of other entrepreneurs, trying to 'sell' and close on a daily basis, there was always a consistent pattern of behaviours where most people would go wrong.

Often this would be right at the start of their conversations with the prospect.

It's also something I used to do early on in my selling and closing days, before I received the proper training and before I had a plan.

It would go something like this…

A prospect would be interested in whatever opportunity or product I was selling at the time, and they'd ask me for more information.

And just like that, I'd jump on a call or video chat with them and *give them all the information.*

They were in control. Not me.

My prospects would say, " So, what does this do?"

"What's the price of this one?"

"How do I go about joining?"

"How much is it?"

"What's this?"

"What's that?"

And guess what? Just like that, I'd give them the information.

Once they had the information, what do you think they did?

They walked away.

They had what they wanted, and I'd never hear from them again.

Don't get me wrong, some people did buy or join, but they were few and far between.

Too many people give away the goods right out the gate, without ever asking the prospect a single question.

This is one of the reasons you're losing the sale.

You have to be in control of the conversation to become a master closer.

Simply giving the prospect what they want is not being in control.

It is your job to give your prospect the information they are asking for *when* you are ready to give it, not when they want it.

They've got to prove to you first, that they're worthy of that information, before you even give it. *(I bet that was something you weren't expecting to read).*

Chapter 5 - The 5 Obstacles We Need To Overcome If We Want To Close The Sale

In order to become a master closer there are 5 factors that need to be overcome, in order to close a sale.

1. Your prospects don't *Know, Like and Trust you yet.* Especially if they're cold prospects (people you've never spoken to before).

I want you to imagine this scenario now, (because it actually happens all time)...

Your prospect asks you for more information.

You jump on a call with them (video chat, face to face meeting, whatever the medium is).

And you instantly give them what they want.

You blurt out all of this information (and most of the time it's too much information that just scares them and leaves them overwhelmed).

Next you jump straight into your pitch.

You go for the sale.

Instantly the *trust is gone, _because it wasn't even established in the first place_*.

This is the same as when people spam their link online.

"Join my opportunity, buy my product, blah blah blah."

Your prospects haven't even had a chance to get to know you yet.

They've not had a chance to get to like you.

And they've definitely not had a chance to get to trust you.

This just pushes the sale further away.

The Quickest way to TRUST is to LISTEN not talk...

What prospects are so used to (and not just when they're having these conversations, but in life too) is not being listened to. *Truly* listened to.

Have you ever noticed that?

This is why this process is so powerful.

Essentially, all you have to do is ask questions (in the right order) and just listen.

Truly listen to your prospect.

If you do this process right, your prospect will be the one doing the most of the talking.

In fact they *should* be the one doing the most talking (this increases the chance of the sale).

Your prospect should be talking 70% of the time.

If you simply listen to your prospect, they are much more likely to trust you.

2. The second obstacle we need to realise and overcome is; *Prospects Withhold Information Or Lie.*

The reason prospects do this is because they don't trust you (yet).

I'll give you an example.

Recently, when I bought my new car, the salesman who was selling me the car (at first) was like a typical car salesman.

He was salesy and direct.

My guard was up from the start.

I didn't trust him.

Because of this lack of trust I withheld information.

I wasn't prepared to show all my cards.

I didn't trust him.

I didn't trust he had *my* best interests at heart.

I want you to think about that scenario for a second, and think how many times have your prospects felt the same?

Like they're just being sold to?

It's surprising isn't it!

Your prospects do the same with you, all the time.

They will withhold information and lie.

Especially if you go straight into your pitch and try to sell them first.

Have you found prospects telling you they haven't got the money?

By the way, that's *never* the reason, as we'll cover further in this book.

Well, have you ever stopped to consider that they may not be telling the truth?

Prospects will especially lie, or withhold information if they feel they are being sold to.

3. *Your prospects don't believe your product/ service or business can help them (yet).*

Think about it for a second. If your prospect was already truly convinced, they'd be buying.

And this does happen. But not as often as we'd like.

Most prospects are asking for more information as they don't yet believe your product/ service/ opportunity, can help them yet.

This is why testimonials, social proof, case studies and word of mouth are so powerful!

They all move the prospect further down the buying line.

However, I'm going to teach you to ask powerful questions that will help your prospects discover for *themselves* how your services can help them.

You may see me mention this a lot.

It's so powerful when your prospect can realise for themselves, discover for themselves, how much they want your service.

Now when I say service, I'm referring to whatever it is you're selling. It really doesn't matter. If you have something to sell, this process works.

Our job is to help the prospect realise how much they want it for themselves.

The easiest way to do this is to ask questions.

4. *Your prospects don't believe in their dreams enough.*

Note: This may refer more to prospects that are looking at joining a business opportunity or a coaching program. Usually linked to purchases / investments of a higher value.

You'd be amazed at the amount of times when I'm on a consultation call with a prospect and I'll say, " So, tell me your 6 to 12 month goals."

And the prospect replies, " Uhmmm."

This is something most people just don't do.

Most people you will find don't think that far ahead.

Some people don't even think about goals and mostly this is because they think they're not achievable.

It's our job to get them to really dream and to picture their dream happening.

We help them to visualise a place where they want to be.

We help them (through questions) to discover for *themselves* what their dreams and goals are.

Now, even though I mentioned earlier that this mainly applies to higher value purchases or investments, it can also be applied to lower ones too.

For example, you sell a weight loss product.

Your prospect probably doesn't think their goal is achievable.

It's our job (through questions) to help them discover what their true goal is, and visualise the end result (that *they* want, this is super important).

Not what you think they want, what they *express to you* they want.

When you really get them to dream and visualise what they want and these things happening for them, they're much more likely to want to buy what it is you're offering.

5. *Your prospects don't believe in themselves enough*

This is perhaps the biggest obstacle of all. It was certainly the one I saw the most.

It comes down to a four letter word. Fear.

Being scared of the unknown.

Afraid to do the things they really want to do.

It is our job (again through questions) to encourage them to believe that they can do this.

Again, this is where testimonials and previous customer comments *really* help.

Especially if you have a testimonial that is similar to your prospect.

It's a great way to help them to believe, and overcome an objection, as you can say, "Well I know someone who thought exactly the same and this is what they had to say…"

That's powerful.

Chapter 6 - Structure Of Your First Consultation Call

Below is the structure of your first consultation call with your prospect.

This is just the outline. We will cover each section individually in the following chapters.

When you're first starting out, it's a good idea to have this outline written down in front of you. It helps you to keep on track with where you're going with the conversation.

It also acts as a good reminder.

- Introduction / Welcome
- Up Front Contract (weed out time-wasters. Super important step)
- Get To Know Them (builds bond, rapport and trust. Helps you discover why they want your product service or opportunity)
- Goals & Dreams (allow them to visualise their dream)

- Reality Check
- Read it back - (Would you agree?)
- Open to take a look? - Send them link to your product/ service/ opportunity/ webinar/ more information / testimonials
- Close the sale - *IF* they're ready
- Schedule a Follow Up - If they're not.

Notice how no-where in that structure do we give away information or give the prospect what they want.

This is not something we simply give-away.

We ask questions to gather information (which I will lay out for you shortly) and we find out why your prospect is interested.

Remember the 5 obstacles we need to overcome to close the sale?

This structure is designed on that.

CHAPTER 7 - EMOTIONAL ROLLERCOASTER & PAIN POINTS

Throughout your first conversation it will be your job to do several things.

If you cover the structure right, you're much more likely to close the sale, build genuine trust with a prospect and have an authentic conversation.

Because, I don't know about you, but give me an authentic conversation over a salesy one, any day of the week!

In fact sales are built on authentic conversations.

Sales is never about tricks and gimmicks.

Further into this book, I will be giving you a set of questions to use and ask, that will help you follow the structure and take your prospect through this conversation.

However it's very important for you to understand *why* you're asking these questions.

It's important for you to understand the reason the structure is the way it is, if you want to become a master closer and make more money.

Emotional Rollercoaster

Throughout your first consultation with your prospect you are going to take the prospect on an emotional rollercoaster.

This needn't sound scary. But it's essential for the sale.

Our questions that we're going to be asking are designed to get your prospect into an emotional state.

That doesn't mean that they're crying in front of you (and I've had that happen to me, on many occasions).

It simply means when your prospect is in an emotional state (emotional frame of mind, they're thinking with their emotions, not logic) they're much more likely to *buy*.

This isn't something new. This is a golden rule of selling.

People buy with emotions.

People don't buy when they're thinking logically. Meaning, "How much is it? What do I have to do to join?"

This stuff does not make people move.

Emotions make people move. Emotions make people buy.

I'll tell you a story about a lady I coached recently.

To give you a little back story, she was looking into a coaching program that was going to help her in her home based business.

The coaching program I was offering (on behalf of another company) was in the region of $3000.

I took her through the structure of the call, asking various questions along the way (which we'll cover shortly) and we arrived at the section where I asked her about her goals and dreams.

She continued to tell me (in her own words) that she wanted to travel with her children.

So I asked her, "When do you want to be able to do that by?"

To which she replied, "This time next year."

So I said, "Why this time next year?"

That was an emotional question.

Meaning, whatever she responded to me at this point, was something that meant a lot to her.

She replied, "Because my children are getting older and they're not going to want to travel with me."

The lady had told me in her own words, not just what her goals and dreams were, but *why* they meant so much to her.

I simply listened and took notes.

The prospect had revealed to me, in her own words, why this was so important.

She was emotionally connected to our conversation at this point.

What this question also allowed the prospect to realise was this.

I need to do something different.

How much more likely do you think that prospect was to investing in the coaching program, compared to if I had just given her a ton of information?

A lot more likely.

Because she did.

And one of the biggest reasons she did, was because I allowed her to realise for herself why she wanted it so bad.

And, she was now, emotionally connected to the conversation and the outcome.

Asking the right questions, listening to your prospect and getting them into an emotional state is critical to becoming a master closer.

Remember, emotions buy.

Pain Points

Just like being in an emotional state, discovering prospects' pain points is also crucial to becoming a master closer.

What is a pain point?

Let's look at the example earlier again.

The lady I was coaching told me her pain points were, she wanted to be able to travel more.

She wanted to be able to travel with her children before they reached a certain age, and no longer wanted to travel with their parents.

My questions allowed her to discover for herself what her pain points were.

(And when I say pain, it doesn't have to mean physical pain, although that can be true at times, it depends what the pain point is).

Another way to look at pain points is what is causing your prospect discomfort.

What keeps them up at night?

What are they not happy with?

Once you help your prospects discover their pain points, you also help them realise *that something needs to change.*

They need a solution.

Your product or service should tie in with the solution.

Let's look at another example.

Let's say you're selling weight loss products.

By asking your prospects the right questions you will help them discover their pain points.

This may look something like this;

"I've lost my confidence and this affects me in other areas of my life."

"I need to do this now to improve my overall health."

"I'm tired of feeling unhappy with the way I look."

These would be considered as prospects pain points.

Now, I know at this point this may be making you feel a tad uncomfortable?

I don't want you to view this as, you are asking questions that will make someone feel sad.

Instead think of it as a way where you're having a real genuine authentic talk with a prospect, where you're listening to their concerns.

Just the fact that you're listening and offering a solution to genuinely help them with something that causes them discomfort, is really something special.

You have a solution.

It's no longer selling.

You have an answer to their problem.

Now, their pain points might not be that 'painful'. It may be something more along the lines of;

"I'm tired of spending money on products that don't work."

The questions inside the Selling Plan don't all have to be applied.

But if you have all the questions in your arsenal, you will truly have a strategy that works every time.

Chapter 8 - Rules To Remember

I know we're covering a lot of ground here, but even if you just take away some of these strategies and start applying them to your conversations, you will see an increase in your sales!

I used to have a little post-it note above my screen when I was doing video chats or consultation calls, with a tip for that week and it always was a great reminder.

Just try them out and see which ones suit you best!

Rule #1 - You want your prospect to be doing most of the talking!

Be honest with yourself.

How many times have you been talking with a prospect where *you're* the one doing the most of the talking?

And if you're used to being the one doing the most of the talking, this habit isn't going to disappear overnight.

You're going to have to remind yourself at times to stop talking.

The person doing the talking is the person who's buying!

Remember this!

If you find that you're talking too much, trying to convince your prospect, just stop and go back to your questions.

I know that sounds blunt, but that's what you need to do.

Your prospect needs to be talking 70% of the time.

You 30%.

That's a big difference!

The more you talk about the feature and benefits, it actually confuses your prospect!

They switch off and they lose interest.

This was a mistake I used to make often. It was like I couldn't get the features and benefits out enough!

I used to give my prospects way too much information, and ultimately scare them off!

Let me tell you the story about the 2 mobile phone sales reps.

1, was a complete newbie to the job.

The other had been in the job a while and was an expert when it came to mobile phones.

Yet, the new guy was completely outselling the expert...

How come?

The expert sales rep (because he knew so much about the phones) just kept giving the customers all this information.

Feature after feature after feature.

Where the new sales rep didn't know anything about the phones in the store yet.

So you know what he did?

He asked questions.

And he kept asking questions.

He would ask things like, "What are you looking for in a mobile phone?"

"What would you like the phone to be able to do?"

And through his questions, he basically was allowing his prospects to *sell themselves* the phone.

He simply offered the one that mostly matched their descriptions.

You might want to read over that story again…

It's a really simple but effective lesson.

Funny how that always seems to be the case, don't you think?

The valuable lesson here is, the more you talk about features and benefits, it confuses the prospect and they don't buy.

The prospect *must* be doing most of the talking.

If you simply take away just this 'rule to remember' here from this book, you will see an increase in your sales.

The 70 % - 30% rule.

Rule #2 - Never, ever convince

If you ever find yourself trying to convince your prospect, stop talking and remember this phrase.

'People buy for THEIR reasons not YOURS'

It is not our job to convince someone, they have to convince themselves.

Have you ever found yourself 'filling the gaps' for your prospects?

Perhaps because you're really knowledgeable about your product or service?

When people fill the gaps you may find yourself trying to convince others.

"This product is amazing because of xyz."

"You should join this opportunity because xyz."

It doesn't matter what you think.

It matters what *they* think.

You might think you have the most amazing product or opportunity in the world, but it ultimately doesn't matter if you don't find out what your prospects' reasons are.

When I first got taught this 'rule', I don't know about you, but it felt like a weight off my shoulders!

I didn't have to convince anymore!

I didn't have to *'sell'*.

All I had to do was ask questions, listen and let the prospect tell me what they wanted.

Rule #3 - Let your prospects discover for themselves.

One of the first questions we ask the prospect in the Selling Plan is;

"What was it about the product/ service/ or opportunity that got you interested?"

This question here is GOLD.

This question does several things;

1. It allows the prospect to tell you the reason why they're interested (no convincing here, they've just told you).
2. It allows your prospect to start to discover for themselves, why they're interested.
3. It allows your prospect to start to convince themselves from the start.
4. Something psychologically happens when a prospect actually *hears themselves* say the reason out loud.
5. You're now able to repeat this reason back to them throughout the conversation.
6. You have a good starting point to knowing what they want and how you can provide the right solution.
7. It saves you time.

Let's just touch on the time aspect a little more here.

Let's say, you didn't ask this question at the beginning of your conversation.

You didn't allow your prospect to discover for themselves.

You could end up talking and talking about a certain feature or benefit that they're not even interested in!

Take a car salesman for example.

Let's assume a prospect goes into a showroom to ask for more information about a new car.

And the sales rep just starts blurting out all these features and benefits about how fast the car is, the in car entertainment system and all this other information. Only to find out at the end, that the prospect was only really interested in the car, because they'd heard it had a good safety reputation and would make a good family car.

Now, if the sales rep had asked the right question at the start, they could have saved themselves so much time talking about what the prospect was *actually* interested in.

Make sense?

Let the prospects discover for themselves.

Let them tell you why they're interested.

CHAPTER 9 - INTRODUCTION AND UP FRONT CONTRACT

Now we've covered the rules to remember, it's time to dive into the actual consultation.

We start with a warm welcome, followed by the Up Front Contract.

Welcome / Introduction

- Don't overthink this
- Keep it short, polite and warm

- Your welcome should be and feel natural (how you would normally welcome someone).

The Up Front Contract

What on earth is an up front contract?

An up front contract serves several purposes and is vital for the beginning of your consultation.

It acts as a kind of agreement, between you and the prospect and allows you to do the following;

Set the agenda

YOU get to set the tone, and tell them what's going to happen.

This is only brief. Like a brief overview of the consultation and what they can expect.

Prospects love it when you give them a brief overview of what to expect! Even if this is more informal.

This also puts you in control from the start.

It gives you the chance to speak first, before your prospect can take over and dominate the conversation.

This is especially important if you are on a schedule.

Specify time

If you are on a schedule, and have only 20 minutes to speak with each prospect, an up front contract will be vital for you to let your prospect know how much time you have together, and for them to respect your time.

This also lets them know, "We can't ramble, as we've only got about 20 minutes."

Look more professional

An upfront contract makes you look so much more professional.

It positions you as the expert and puts your prospects at ease, knowing they are talking to someone who knows what they're talking about!

Permission to say yes and no

At the very beginning of the call we're going to give our prospects permission to say no.

What this means is, we'll give them permission to say, this isn't for them.

Now obviously, we don't want our prospects to say, this isn't for them. But wouldn't you rather they told you that at the very beginning, than hours down the line?

Especially if this is a higher value close we're talking about.

One that also requires a certain level of commitment.

I want to challenge you to become comfortable with a 'no'.

To look at a 'no' differently.

When I got taught this concept it was liberating!

I remember my trainer saying to me, "Emma, when someone tells you no, that is actually a win in my book."

I remember thinking, "Errmmm how?" As obviously I wanted all my prospects to be yes's.

My trainer then said, 'Because a 'no' means you can move on. What you don't want Emma is *I'll think about it.*"

I'll let you ponder that for a second…

See, when you get told no it allows you to draw a line under that prospect and move on.

It is a completed outcome.

Where as a 'think about it' leaves you in no man's land, uncertain.

A no also allows you to ask for a *referral.*

Whenever you get a no you should always be asking for a referral.

You can say, " Okay, great. Do you know anybody who would love this product? Or, could you give me the name of someone who you think this would be a great fit for?"

Always ask for the referral.

If you don't, you're leaving money on the table.

CHAPTER 10 - UPFRONT CONTRACT EXAMPLE

After we've welcomed the client we move onto the Upfront Contract.

Below is an example of my exact version, which you can use as your own, or model it and make changes. Making it feel more like you.

In fact, I strongly advise you to tweak this so it feels more authentic, more like 'you'.

When I introduced this into my calls, I started making *way* more sales.

The reason for this being; from the very beginning of the call I'm setting the agenda and I let people know what to expect.

Up Front Contract Example:

" Hey welcome to the call. How are you today?

Usually these consultations take about 20 minutes.

The intention of today's consultation is, I want to get to know more about you and where you're at right now.

It's really important before we move any further forward that we see if this is a right fit for you, as our opportunity/ product isn't for everyone and I really want you to be sure that more importantly this is a right fit for you.

Are you ok with me asking some questions? (Yes)

Great! Ok, so typically how this call goes is, I'll ask you several questions to help you to see if this is a right fit for you and then at the end of the call, if it makes sense, we can look at you joining us if it's a right fit or I can send you some more information. How does that sound?"

Now again, you do not need to use this verbatim.

You can change it so it suits your style/ and the product or service you're offering.

Let's break it down.

- As you can see I specify the time the call typically takes. If you get someone that likes to ramble, saying this at the very beginning of the call helps them to realise they can't take up too much time rambling. We need to stick to the agenda.
- Saying, " The intention of today's consultation is I want to get to know more about you and where you're at right now." This lets your prospect know that you're going to be asking them questions and it prepares them to know what to expect.
- There is a specific part in the Up Front Contract where the sale is initially made. It potentially sets you up for the sale from the start. This is the section; "It's really important before we move any further forward that we see if this is a right fit for

you, as our opportunity/
product/service isn't for everyone."

When I first got taught this concept I
remember thinking, "I can't say that!" It
sounded too negative.

However, what this phrase actually does is,
it gives your prospect an option.

It allows them to see that you're not just
after the 'sale'. This is going to build *trust*
with your prospect.

What this phrase also does is it acts like a
take-away.

Have you ever heard of the phrase, 'take-
away' within sales and selling before?

What this means is, when you take
something away from someone, they want it
more.

A bit like a child.

So, by saying, "This product isn't for
everyone," in your prospects mind they start
to think, "Well I want it for me!"

I remember feeling uncomfortable with the thought of using this phrase at the beginning of my calls, and perhaps you are to.

I remember thinking, "I can't say that! Why would I want to say to someone, 'Hey, this might not be for you?"

It felt too negative.

However, I invite you to try it on.

When I started using this phrase at the beginning of my calls, guess what my prospects started doing?

They upped their game.

They started selling themselves to me!

All of a sudden my prospects were trying so much harder to convince me that they were a right fit, or that they wanted it.

Imagine that for a second.

You haven't even really started your conversation and your prospect is ready to sell themselves to you!

- By saying, "Are you okay with me asking you some questions?" You're giving your prospects their first chance to say *yes*.

That first yes is really important as you're giving your prospects the first opportunity to say yes to you. The more you can get your prospect to say yes, the more likely they'll say yes at the end.

It also builds trust (and we know how important that is by now, yes?) as you are asking for their permission to ask questions.

- By saying, "*Great! Ok, so typically how this call goes is, I'll ask you several questions to help you to see if this is a right fit for you and then at the end of the call, if it makes sense, we can look at you joining us if it's a right fit or I can send you some more information. How does that sound?*"

This final part of the upfront contract again just sets the agenda for the call.

It helps your prospects to feel at ease when they know what to expect.

You're also planting the seed that at the end of the call they can either join, or you can send them some more information.

This is setting up the right expectations and it also lets you steer the conversation towards a useful outcome.

We're not saying to clients at this point, "At the end of the call you can go away and have a think about it."

That is not a useful outcome.

You ideally either want them to make a decision, yes or no, or that you will send more information and then schedule a follow up.

If you leave your prospect to go away and 'think about it' you are lowering your chances of the sale.

- You end the up front contract with *'How does that sound?'* This builds trust again, as you're getting permission from your prospect that what you've just outlined is ok.

I've never once had a prospect say, "No this doesn't sound good."

They all say, "Yes, that's great," or something along those lines.

They answer me almost like they're ready for me to start asking the questions and they're ready to sell themselves to me!

As you can see, there's many layers to the Upfront Contract.

Don't be afraid to give it a try.

It may feel awkward at first.

Like everything, it will take time for it to feel natural.

However, if you keep practicing this, I promise you, it changes the *entire* conversation.

If you get it right, you truly are giving yourself the best start, and the best chances of closing the sale right out the gates.

This is why the Upfront Contract is so important and it really is a game-changer.

CHAPTER 11 - THE SELLING PLAN - QUESTION 1

Question: "What was it about the product/or opportunity that got you interested?"

As we dive into the questions, it's important to note;

1. They are to be asked in this order.

2. They do not have to be word-for-word like the examples I'm giving you. They can be changed slightly, but keep to the structure.

I absolutely love this question.

This question gives you the information that will allow you to close the sale.

Well, I should say, increases your chance of closing the sale.

Instead of you spending most of your time on the call telling your prospect all the different amazing things your product or service does, how about they get to tell you from the very start?

This very first question tells you their reasons, not yours.

Even if you just start asking this question with your prospects and apply nothing else from this book… you will increase your chances of closing the sale.

It's important to take notes at this point (as you're going to repeat their words back to them throughout the conversation).

This is where they may reveal to you what their *pain point* is, also.

Write it down.

This question allows you, instantly to know what their reason is.

What their pain point is.

What's their motivation?

This is why this question is so powerful.

Forget convincing! Get them to tell you.

PRO TIP : Throughout the entire process, take notes. The notes that you write down will help you to close the sale. You will repeat the words back to them when we come to the close. And we always use their words, <u>never</u> yours.

PRO TIP EXAMPLE: I was coaching a client just recently, and because I've used this process for such a long time now, I tend to recognise patterns in people's language when they're talking to me.

People tend to use the same word over and over.

Have you ever noticed that? (I do it too).

I will make a note of that word, because when I repeat it back to them, it's like I'm speaking their language.

This will help you to close the sale.

Back to the client.

She kept saying to me, "I really just want to feel comfortable. I want a comfortable life. I want to feel comfortable with my finances..." She kept using the word, 'comfortable'.

So I made a note of it.

I made sure to use the word comfortable, frequently, when talking back with her.

This allowed me to speak her language and mirror her.

I also took many more notes of *exactly what she was saying to me,* so when I recapped our call at the end of the conversation she said, "Oh my word! Would you send me what you've just said to me? That was powerful, hearing that being said back to me!"

She said, "I've always had these thoughts in my mind, but hearing them said to me like that has really just registered."

I'd hit an emotional chord and was able to connect with her on a really deep level.

All I did was repeat back to her *what she'd already said to me.*

It also proves you're listening.

Which in turn increases trust.

And remember, when someone is thinking with emotion, they are much more likely to buy!

CHAPTER 12 - QUESTION 2

The following questions are designed to get to know your prospect.

This section is all about getting to know them!

There are several questions you can use here, and they all depend on what your prospect gave as an answer to your first question.

Examples:

Question : "Tell me more about that"

Question : "What does a typical day/month in your life look like?"

Question: "What's really important to you at the minute?"

The second set of questions is all about you becoming a detective!

It is your job to find out as much information as possible about what they just told you.

The trick is to dig deeper!

PRO TIP: Imagine an onion. You need to peel the layers! 'Tell me more about that' is the perfect question to ask that allows you to peel the onion, and dig deeper.

More examples of Questions to ask for Question 2:

Question: "What is it about what you just told me that's important to you?"

- This is a great question to follow up with from the first, as you are instantly peeling the onion. This demands an internal, emotional response and remember what we

covered in the previous chapters? When your prospect is in an emotional state of mind they are more likely to **buy.**

Question: "What would you love to change?"

Question: "What do you do for a living?"

Question: "What do you enjoy about your job?"

Question: "What don't you enjoy about your job?"

Question: "What products are you currently using or have you used in the past?"

Question: "What is it you're looking for in the service?"

I could go on and on with a list of questions for Question 2 of the Selling Plan.

It really is your job at this point to just act like a detective and find out more about your prospect.

The questions asked at this stage of The Selling Plan, will highly depend on what was said in response to the first question you asked.

The only way you will hone the skill of knowing what question/s to ask for question 2, is by practice.

Sharpening the skill.

The more you do this and you practice, the better you will become at knowing what to ask for this section.

PRO TIP: You can ask several questions at this section. As long as you are 'peeling the onion' and getting to know more about your prospect, no question is a silly one.

CHAPTER 13 - QUESTION 3

Ok, by this stage you should know a little more about your prospects.

You're building trust, building rapport and by now they should be used to being asked questions.

You are firmly in control.

But your prospect is enjoying you being in control, and also enjoying being *listened* to.

Now it's time to allow your prospect to look ahead.

It's time to help them dream.

It's time to guide them to talk about their goals.

It's time to help them visualise the result / outcome they want (however big or small this may be).

Remember, we are on an emotional rollercoaster and it's very important your prospect goes through the different stages.

Emotions = Buying State = Sales

PRO TIP: If your prospect can picture themselves getting the result / outcome they want they are much more likely to buy.

Dreaming and visualising their future (however small or big this may be) is important.

The more your prospect can <u>visualize</u> and start to feel what it would be like to achieve what they want, the more they will want it.

There are several questions you can ask at this stage and again they will depend on what they have already told you.

Question Examples:

Question: "Where would you love to be in 6 months time?"

Question: "What would you love to change about your current situation?"

Question: "What results are you looking for?"

Question: "What are your goals for the next 6 to 12 months?"

Example: Let's imagine you own a gym or you're selling a weight loss programme/ or product and you ask.

"What's your goals for the next 6 months?" and they say.

"Well, I really want to lose X amount in the next 6 months."

You could follow up with.

"What would you love to change about your current health situation to help you get there?"

"What would you love to change about where you are now with your health?"

"What would be the perfect outcome for you and your health in 6 months time?"

Can you see how each question is all about your prospect.

Peeling the onion.

You are getting to know so much more about them!

<u>All you have to do is tailor what you have to offer, to suit their needs!</u>

You may want to re-read that last sentence again.

Important reminder: All the time they are talking, you are writing down their answers. In their words! (If you are having a face to face meeting, you can still use a notepad and explain that you'd like to make sure you make a note of everything they want).

This is vitally important. This is never about your interpretation of what they want. Or you suggesting what you think is best for them. Let them tell you. You're simply providing a solution (if it fits).

Another reason you will want to take notes and write this down is because you're going to remind them of this information. It is a powerful process when you read your prospect back their answers in their own words.

This is so much more powerful than simply listing and naming benefits and features.

I hope you're starting to see that now!

CHAPTER 14 - QUESTION 4

You've asked your prospect what their goals are.

What they'd love to change.

Where they'd like to be in 6 to 12 months time.

What results they're looking for.

We've helped them to visualise what they want, and tell us what they want.

Now it's time for us to discover what *really* motivates them.

What's the *real* reason they want, what they've just told you they want.

This next question reveals the *true* motivating factors behind what they want.

This is truly their **why**!

Question Examples:

Question: "How would your life change if you achieved xxx?"

Question: "How would your life change if you were making enough money to quit your job?"

Question: "How would you feel if you achieved xxx?"

Question: "How would you feel in 6 months time if you xxx?"

Question: "How would it feel to get those results?"

Notice how the questions are all based around *feelings*.

<u>People buy for emotional reasons.</u>

Let me go back to some of my coaching client examples, to help solidify the reason behind why we ask this question.

A lot of the time when I was talking with a prospect they would tell me all these *monetary things*.

They'd say;

'I want to make 5000 a month.'

'I want to make 10,000 a month.'

'I want to advance in my business.'

'I want to get to the next level.'

Or one of the most frequent answers I always had was,

'I want financial freedom.'

Almost everyone used to say this.

As soon as they said this I would reply;

'Okay, great. What does financial freedom look like to you?'

Or, 'Great. What is it about 5000 a month that would make a difference for you?'

They'd be stumped.

There would be a little pause.

They'd never thought about it like this before.

People get so hung up on the outcome, or the monetary goal they don't actually stop to think why it is they want it.

When you ask this question you get to the real reasons.

It's never about the money.

It's never about the product.

It's about the reason behind that.

And this question will reveal it for you and more importantly for your prospect.

This is why this question is probably one of the most important questions you'll ask within the Selling Plan.

It's about what you get as a result of achieving X.

Make sense?

Let's look at the weight loss example again;

You could ask.

'How would your life change if you lost XX in 6 months time?'

'How would you feel if you lost XXX?'

These are such emotional questions (in a good way).

This is the motivating factor.

You will usually find their responses will go something like this;

'Oh my goodness! I'd feel amazing!'

'I'd finally have my confidence back!'

'It would be such a relief!'

Your prospect may get a little emotional.

It all depends on what it is you're selling.

This is totally ok!

You are helping them to discover what it is they really want.

And you are also helping them to go after it!

As humans this is what really motivates us.

At times we may think it's the 5000 a month, or the monetary materialist things but it's usually a lot deeper than that.

PRO TIP: Again, please remember to make a note of their answer to this question as you will repeat it back to them shortly.

CHAPTER 15 - QUESTION 5

It's important to note here that your prospect may already be in a position to buy.

At this point they may be ready for the close.

After all you've just helped them discover how much they really want your product or service!

If this is the case, don't worry about going further just go straight to the close and close them, as you normally would any other prospect.

Do not continue to try and 'sell them'.

Do not get in the way of the sale (I'll explain more on this in the Sabotaging The Sale chapter).

If your prospect isn't quite there yet, that's ok.

This next question is testing their commitment to buy.

It can also be used as a soft close.

You're just testing the waters to see if they're serious about buying and getting the result they just told you they want.

Question Examples:

Question: "How committed are you to making this happen?"

Question: "Is this something you can see yourself doing / buying?"

Remember, at this point they have already told you what their reason of interest was.

What their goals are.

And with the previous question, they've told you the real motivating factor behind why they want what you have to offer.

Your prospect has been selling themselves to you this whole time.

Your prospect is qualifying themselves to you with every question thus far in the Selling Plan process.

Not once have you given them more information.

Not once have <u>you</u> tried to sell them.

This is the beauty of this process.

It allows you to sell authentically.

Now, it's also really important to point out at this point that your prospect will be enjoying this process.

I have done this process enough times to know.

Think about it;

1. Your prospect is being heard.

2. They may be sharing real, personal information with you that has a deep meaning for them (again this all depends on what you have to offer)
3. They're sharing information about their life that makes a big difference to them.
4. They may have never spoken to anyone previously about the things they're sharing with you. This is mostly because they've possibly never been asked these types of questions before, and also because you are actually listening to them. They are not used to this.
5. Your prospects are so familiar with being 'sold' to.
6. This process allows your prospect to discover for themselves the real reasons why they want your product or service.

Moving on.

When you ask your prospect, "And how committed are you to making this happen?"

This is another question where your prospect is selling themselves to you.

The answer to this question is usually a good indicator as to how well motivated your prospect is, and how much they want what you have to offer.

Your previous question allowed your prospect to realise how much more they actually want this.

Now it's time to get some commitment.

You do not want time wasters.

You do not want tire kickers.

Hopefully you weeded out the time wasters at the very beginning.

However this question can also act like another qualifying question.

A check in point to see if your prospect is still serious.

The answer to this question will allow you to help your prospect, and *remind them* of how committed they are when it comes to the close.

PRO TIP: Remember at the very beginning, we said that one of the reasons why people won't buy or join is because they don't believe in themselves enough yet?

When you write down the answer to this question (in their words), and they've said, "I'm so committed. I need to make this change."

When you arrive at the close, if your prospect has even the slightest sign of cold feet, you simply repeat their words back to them and you remind them, "You can do this because you said this to me…remember?"

Also, if you get a bit of a wishy-washy answer here, this could be an indication that your prospect might not be suitable.

They might not be a right fit.

Their answer will tell you whether they're serious or not.

You do not want to invest a lot of time into someone who's simply not committed to their dreams.

Again, this does depend on what you are selling.

This question might not be appropriate for every scenario.

Perhaps for smaller transactions.

But if you need commitment from your prospect, do not be afraid to ask this question.

Get the commitment from your prospect.

Let's look at the weight loss example again.

Let's say your prospect wants to lose x amount before their wedding in 12 months time, and you're offering them the opportunity to work with you one on one to get the results.

You 100% want someone who is going to commit and not waste your time.

I can't tell you the amount of people I have coached over the years who have invested so much time into a prospect and that prospect was simply not serious from the word go.

I used to do this myself, prior to learning and applying these skills!

I would not like to think of the amount of time I invested in prospects who were not committed from the start.

The Selling Plan not only teaches you to become a master closer.

It helps you weed out the time wasters too.

CHAPTER 16 - QUESTION 6

Ok, now it's time for a reality check.

In the previous questions we've asked our prospects, we've guided them to dream.

To share their goals.

What they want in the next 6 to 12 months.

The results they want.

We've guided them to imagine what it would feel like to achieve those results.

Whatever they are. Big or small.

We've even helped them to tell us how much they want it.

How committed they are.

At this point your prospect is on an emotional high.

They feel good.

They're visualising achieving what they want.

But prospects don't tend to buy at this point.

<u>We need to help them to realise something.</u>

And that's why this next question is designed to bring them crashing back down with a reality check.

It sounds harsh.

But it's a vitally important step of the process.

We need them to realise that what they're doing at this moment in time isn't helping them achieve what they've just shared with us.

If it was they wouldn't be speaking with you.

We need to help them realise they need to do something different.

They need to change.

This question is the transition for your prospect.

This is where they realise (for themselves), "Wow, I need this more than I realised I do. I need that product more than I realised I do, because look at the goals I've just laid out."

It is time for a reality check.

Not to be harsh.

Because it's our job to help our prospects.

It's our job to help them achieve their goals.

It's our job to help them see the truth.

That something needs to change.

Your Mindset Around Selling: *If you have a product or a service, or whatever it is you sell that you believe in.*

That you're passionate about.

That genuinely makes a difference for people.

It is your purpose, your job to share that with people.

This is the difference between selling and providing solutions for people.

If you can switch your mindset around what you sell to serving people instead you will close more sales.

You will also have so much more fulfillment.

It's about providing solutions.

Genuinely helping people.

If you have a product or service that does that, it's your role to share it.

Moving on.

So, your prospect is on an emotional high and we're about to bring them back down with a reality check.

We need to help them realise that what they're doing at the moment isn't working or that they need to make a change *and* that your product or service can genuinely help them.

Question Examples;

Question: "What do you feel is your biggest challenge when you're trying to achieve X?"

Question: "What's your biggest challenge when you're trying to lose weight?"

Question: "What's your biggest challenge when you're trying to become more healthy?"

Question: "What's your biggest challenge in your current job?"

Question: "What is it about your current job that you want to change?"

Question: "What is it about your current habits that you want to change?"

Question: "What is it about your current finances that you want to change?"

Or whatever it is your prospect has just been talking to you about.

There's a lot of variations to this question, but basically you want to find out what's challenging them.

What's not working?

We want to get to the pain point.

If you can't get your prospect emotionally connected to their pain point, you will struggle to make the sale.

Recap: So again, just to recap this chapter and question.

We are on an emotional rollercoaster.

We've just experienced the highs.

Now it's time to bring your prospect back down to reality.

To help them realise this is the current situation.

We've dreamed (which is vital and so important to help your prospect to visualize and to start to believe it's possible).

But it's also now vitaly important to look at reality.

What is happening right now.

To have authentic conversations with your prospect.

So they can see for themselves something needs to change.

Special Masterclass

The Selling Plan:

Over 4 x hours of recorded training from Emma.

Would you love access to a pre-recorded Live webinar that Emma held covering the Selling Plan in detail? Including a special 2 x hour bonus training on overcoming objections?

Get access to Emma's training:

The Proven Step-By-Step Selling Plan To Close More Clients & Make More Sales

Including special bonus 2 x hour training on Overcoming Objections

Get All The Details Here:

The Selling Plan Special Masterclass

pagecreatorpro.com/nuyouuk/the-selling-plan/

CHAPTER 17 - QUESTION 7

Our next set of questions are designed to dig deeper into the prospects pain.

We're searching for more information about the pain.

What worries your prospect?

What keeps them up at night?

What do they want to change?

Can your product or service provide a solution to that pain?

We start with this question;

Question: "On a scale of 1 to 10, (1 being very unhappy), how happy and satisfied are you with X?"

Question Examples;

Question: 'On a scale of 1 to 10, how happy and satisfied are you with your current skincare regime?'

Question: 'On a scale of 1 to 10, how happy and satisfied are you with your current health and weight goals?'

Question: 'On a scale of 1 to 10, how happy and satisfied are you with your current finances?'

Question: 'On a scale of 1 to 10, how happy and satisfied are you with your job?'

<u>We immediately follow this question (once they've given us the answer) with the following question below;</u>

Question: 'Tell me more about that'

'Tell me more about that,' allows you to peel the onion.

To dig deeper.

It really is a great question to have in your arsenal, that you can use at several points in the conversation.

It also allows your prospect to reveal how they are emotionally attached to the pain/problem.

Emotions = Sale

Let's look at an example.

Let's imagine you've asked, "On a scale of 1 to 10 (1 being very unhappy), how happy and satisfied are you with your current weight loss goals?"

And your prospect says, "Oh, I'm a 1."

You say, "Tell me more about that. What was your reason for giving it a 1?"

Prospect, "Well, because I've been like this for so long and I need to make a change."

With this scenario, we are getting closer to the pain points.

*We are also agitating it a little bit because this is what will make your prospect **move towards making a buying decision.***

PRO TIP: Let's look at the word agitating here for a second. It's vital that your prospect is not comfortable during this stage of the selling process.

Now that doesn't mean that your prospect should be really uncomfortable, that is not our role. Our role is to help them to realise something needs to change.

It's our role to help them realise this for themselves.

We want them to see that 'What you're doing at the moment isn't providing you the results you want.'

Again, they wouldn't be here speaking to you if that was the case.

They have some kind of pain (problem)

They're looking for the solution (you, your product or service)

These questions are all designed for you to be able to provide the perfect, tailored solution to their problem.

Let's look at another scenario;

Let's imagine you've asked, "On a scale of 1 to 10, how happy and satisfied are you with your current finances?"

Your prospect says, "3."

You say, "Can you tell me more about that? What was the reason for giving me a 3?"

They say, "Well, we get by, but we only just about make enough money to pay the bills. We don't get any spare money to go on holiday and do things with the children."

Can you see in the scenario above how you've uncovered the pain?

This is why this prospect wants more help with their finances. They don't simply want to 'make more money,' they want to be able to breathe every month knowing they have more money left over after paying the bills.

They want to be able to have more flexibility in their finances so they can go on holiday and do more things with the children.

This is their pain.

The problem that keeps them awake at night.

The problem that agitates them.

The problem that worries them.

The problem they want fixed.

The solution they are searching for.

Are you/ what you offer, the solution?

Remember: Continue to take notes. Your prospect is doing all the talking here. You are simply asking the questions, digging deeper and peeling the onion.

You are also guiding this conversation and helping them to make an informed decision.

Your questions truly will be helping your prospect.

It's important to pause for a second and note here, you may not use all the questions in the Selling Plan Process.

You may not need to dig so deep.

It all depends on the problem.

The pain, the size of it, and also the price point of what you're selling.

The higher the price point the more this process is vital.

You will need to dig deep and be a detective on the questions if you are selling a product or service that has a high price point.

So to recap you may not need to dig so deep, but you still need your prospect to be telling you the reasons why they're interested in your products or opportunity.

CHAPTER 18 - QUESTION 8

You've covered your prospects interests.

You've covered their goals and dreams.

You've touched on their pain points and really helped them to discover why they want what you have.

Now it's time to uncover the first possible glimpse at an objection.

This next question is designed to reveal any possible objections.

What this allows you to do is, address it before it even becomes a real objection.

It allows you to squash it flat to stop it from resurfacing again.

This also gives you a heads up!

It allows you to see what the objection could be *before* you get to the close (so you can be prepared for it, if it needs to be addressed further).

Question: "What do you feel is the biggest factor that would stop you from X?"

Further examples;

Question: 'What do you feel is this biggest factor that would stop you from making this change?'

Question: 'What do you feel is this biggest factor that would stop you getting from where you are now to where you want to be?'

Question: 'What do you feel is this biggest factor that would stop you from achieving your goal you just shared with me?'

Question: 'What do you feel is this biggest factor that would stop you from getting the results you want? (You can repeat their words back to them in this question)'

We also have a little insight into their intentions at this point, before we've even closed them.

Some prospects might say, "Well, I just don't know if I've got the time to do this."

Or, "Well, I don't know if I'll have the finances to do this."

Or, "I don't know if I'll have the money."

<u>You are getting an insight into their possible objection.</u>

Let's look at the weight loss scenario again;

Let's imagine the prospect says, "I just can't do it on my own. I feel like if I keep having to do this by myself, then I'm just going to go back to my old ways."

Instantly here, you can be thinking of the solution and tailoring your solution to the prospects pain point.

You could say, "Well, great! I'm pleased you said that because we have a community of people all working towards the same goals. We also have a program that is group focussed. Do you think if you were part of this community and group and you were plugged in with all these other people who have similar goals, you'd much more like to stay on track?"

You can even insert a customer testimonial at this point who had a similar pain point to your prospect.

Can you also see how you've just tailored your solution to their problem?

You will have also potentially squashed the objection, making the close and sale easier.

Another really common response I used to get when coaching business clients (who were searching for coaching and mentorship to take their businesses to 6 figures and beyond) was this;

I would ask, "What do you feel is the biggest factor that would stop you from making this change?"

And they would answer, "Ermm, probably me."

Then they would go on to say things like;

"I don't tend to stick at anything."

"I find it hard to concentrate and stay motivated."

"I know I tend to get in my own way."

"I overthink everything."

"I can't make decisions."

At this point I often used to throw in an additional question where I would ask;

"Do you feel like if you had a coach or a mentor or if you were part of a supportive community that were encouraging you, it would help you?"

The answer was almost always, "Yes."

Can you see how I was seeding in the solution with our product and services to their problem?

The questions in the Selling Plan allow you to get straight to the prospect's pain, straight to the problem and for you to offer the correct, individually tailored solution.

You only talk about solutions that matter to *them*.

This is what is going to move the needle.

This is what is going to increase your chances of closing the sale.

CHAPTER 19 - QUESTION 9

Now at this point you may be thinking,
'Wow, this is a lot of questions!'

Like I mentioned earlier, you do not need to
use them all.

You can use a variety of them.

You will find ones that work best for you.

Some may not be necessary.

However, I highly, highly recommend you try them out.

Every question, at least a few times.

Just try it on.

Try it out, see whether it works for you.

You may feel uncomfortable.

This is completely normal when trying something new.

The only way you will get better at asking these questions and become a master closer is with *practice.*

This next question is probably the <u>biggest</u> reality check of them all.

Question: "What is the cost to you for not fixing these problems?"

With this question you are basically saying, "Ok, so if you don't make a change, what is the cost to you for not doing something different?'

Again, this all depends on the context of what it is you're selling.

When I was selling coaching and mentorship programs that allowed business owners to build a thriving business online, often I'd get responses similar to this one;

"Well, the cost is, I continue going to a job that I hate and it's affecting my health because I'm so stressed in my job."

Or, "I'm so stressed because of my finances and the debt that I'm in."

As you can see the cost isn't just monetary.

This question is so powerful because again, it grounds them, it's a reality check.

It reminds your prospect why they want to make a change and reminds them they *need* to make a change.

Rule To Remember: For most human beings it's hard to make a change. We fear change.

Have you ever noticed that?

This is why, for a lot of your prospects they will struggle to make a decision.

Fear of the unknown.

Fear of making a bad investment.

Fear of success even!

I could write another book on this subject alone.

The point is, you will need to guide them.

It's your job to help them.

Especially for those prospects who struggle with change and making decisions.

They need a little helping hand.

A little guidance.

Almost like a little encouraging nudge.

This is your role.

You can also go one step further with this question and ask;

Question: "What is the cost to you over 5 years if you don't fix these problems?"

Question: "What is the cost to you over 5 years if you don't fix (insert what they've told you)?"

This is when things really hit home.

Especially if your prospect is wanting to make a significant change.

If you were to say to someone, 'Ok, so if you carried on doing the same things that you're doing now, what does your future look like in 5 years time?' That is a scary question.

If the pain or problem is strong enough, when your prospect thinks of being in exactly the same place as where they are now in 5 years time, that will really hit home.

If this doesn't make your prospect move towards a buying decision nothing will.

Again, we're not here to scare prospects but it is our job to help them.

And in order to help them you need to be able to have authentic conversations and help them to realize for themselves that something needs to change.

"What is the cost to you for not fixing these problems?"

"What's the cost to you over time?"

"What's the cost to you over 5 years if you don't change?"

"What's your life going to look like in 5 years time if it stays the same?"

Prospects don't even want to contemplate thinking of this.

Now your prospects really should be in a position to move forward.

This is the transition to buy.

CHAPTER 20 - TRANSITION

This now brings us into the transition.

You've really taken your prospect through an emotional roller coaster (in a good way).

And yet we still haven't given them any information (this is a good thing by the way).

Remember, you are in control!

You set the agenda.

Your prospect has to qualify themselves first and show they're a good fit.

By doing this, your prospect is going to want what you have, way more!

Because look at the process they've just been through.

Look at the questions you've asked.

You've helped your prospect to discover that they actually want your product or service, and I mean, really want it!

Yes, at the beginning they told you the initial reasons (with our first question) however, now your prospect will be thinking, 'I really *do* want this!'

Or, 'Maybe, I really *do* need to take a closer look at this!'

Or, 'Wow!I want this more than I realized!'

You've asked authentic questions.

You've listened.

Your prospects have been heard.

Your prospects may have shared some deep personal information.

Undoubtedly, at this point the trust between you and your prospect will have increased tenfold.

Think about it, whenever you've shared personal information that is centred around your emotions with someone else, and they've listened to you. Not judged. Just listened. Didn't you feel some sense of connection with that individual?

Did you feel you could trust that individual more?

That is how your prospect will be feeling towards you, if you've done this right.

And that is a *special* place to be.

This can create customers for life.

And we've covered that trust leads to a higher probability of making the sale.

You've allowed them to get *real and vulnerable.*

You've allowed them to rediscover their dreams and you've helped them connect it to their pains.

They are emotionally connected at this point.

IMPORTANT NOTE: If you feel at this point that you can close your prospect, <u>close them.</u>

<u>*If you have a sense that you could close your prospect, now is a good time to do it.*</u>

With practice you will start to know when the time is right.

You will see and hear it in your prospects tone of voice, what they're saying and their body language.

As you become a master closer you will know when the time is right to close.

Transition continued:

At this point you simply say;

"Okay. So, what I've just heard is…" <u>and you literally repeat everything they've just said to you (in their words).</u>

Let's imagine again it's the weight loss example. You could say;

"Okay, so, from what you've just told me what got you interested in the product is you're trying to lose X amount of weight, because you're going on holiday in September. And you've just told me that you've been trying to do it on your own but you really struggle. And one of the biggest challenges you face is you just need some help and motivation, you can't do it by yourself. You also said, you're sick and tired of being the weight that you are, it's affected your confidence and you're really ready for a change."

All you have done here is repeated what they've already told you, back to them.

And this is powerful.

Do not underestimate how powerful it is to hear your own words spoken back to you.

Let's also look at what else happens here;

1. It shows that you've listened and paid attention to what your prospect was telling you.
2. It increases trust. Your prospect will be thinking, "Wow, they really did

pay attention to me. I like this person. I trust this person."

3. Your prospect should now be in 'The Buying Zone'.

CHAPTER 21 - THE BUYING ZONE

At this stage your prospect should be in the buying zone.

This simply means they are either very close to buying, or they're already ready to buy.

To recap, you've just read back to them everything they've shared to you through the Selling Plan questions.

(You were able to do this because you took notes).

You are then simply going to ask;

Question: *"Would you agree that there is a gap between where you are now and where you want to be?"*

And your prospect will answer "Yes."

This is the transition.

Note: You can ask a variable of questions at this point as long as it concludes with a 'Yes or No' answer.

If you have done this right 99% of the time it should be a yes!

This is where you either close them, or you send them more information.

Question examples;

Question: "Would you like to hear how our product/service can help you?"

Question: "Would you like me to quickly tell you about our product and how it can help you? Then we can look to get you started?"

Question: "Would you like some more information at this point or are you ready to get started?"

Question: "Would you like some information about how we can help you?"

Question: "Would you like me to share some information about how our product/service helped another client of mine?"

Question: "Would you like more information so you can see how my product/service will help you get (insert their results)?"

Question: "Are you happy for me to tell you a little bit more about (insert product or service) and quickly show you how it can help you (insert their goals/results they want/what they've just shared)?

The point is here that you can now totally tailor this question to your prospects needs.

<u>If you are going to talk about your product or service or send them more information you now know what features or benefits to focus on that are specific to what your prospect just told you!</u>

Don't start to talk about information that isn't relevant!

CHAPTER 22 - CLOSE

Back in my early days of selling. I used to be so concerned with this part of the process.

I'd take my prospects through all the questions, have real connections with them, authentic conversations.

Then I'd worry about what to say to close them.

I thought there was some magic way of doing it.

Some super ninja way.

And the truth is, there isn't.

It's just one simple question.

The only close question you ever need to ask is...

"What should happen next?"

Or

"What would you like to happen next?"

That's it!

Don't shy away from the sale.

When you want to tie it down, ask, "What should happen next?"

And your prospect will tell you.

CHAPTER 23 - POWER OF TESTIMONIALS

If you are not looking to send more information to your prospect at this point it is a great transition to include a testimonial.

If you can sense they are not quite ready to close, a testimonial really can make all the difference (especially if it's a personal one).

If it's not your own testimonial (the most powerful) you want to try and match a testimonial to the situation your prospect has just described to you.

Can you think of a previous client, or someone on your team or just another instance, when you've been able to help someone similar to the prospect you are speaking to now?

The transition looks like this;

You: "Would you agree there's a gap between where you are now and where you want to be?"

"Yes."

"Great! Well, let me just tell you a little bit about my friend, X. She was in exactly the same situation that you're in now. She wanted to lose X amount by X amount of time because she was going on holiday for her friend's wedding. And I remember her sharing with me that she just couldn't do it by herself, she'd been trying for years. She'd also used so many products and got nowhere and she was really unhappy and desperate to change. She came to me, tried our products and joined our community where we all help each other and all share what's working. Within 6 months, she'd lost X and achieved her goal of X."

Sharing a testimonial that is very similar to what your prospect wants is very powerful.

It shows them that if someone else can do it who had the same pain points and challenges they do, so can they.

The closer the match the better.

Like I previously said, if this can be *your* testimonial (if you find similarities between their story and yours) this is even more powerful!

As they've already gained trust in you. So the testimonial becomes even more believable.

Only share a testimonial at this point if you are going for the close.

If you feel your prospect is ready to close, do it.

CHAPTER 24 - TRANSITION CONTINUED

Another great transition question at this point to move your prospect closer to the sale is this;

Question: *"Are you open to considering X as the answer to fill that gap?*

Or,

Question: "Are you open to taking a look at X as the answer to X?"

Whenever I've asked this question at this stage I've never had a single prospect say 'no'.

This is because throughout your process they've discovered how much they want it!

It is now vital that you give your prospect EXACT details of what is going to happen next.

Set your prospect up with the right expectations.

They need to know what is going to happen next.

Example;

"Okay, next I'm going to send you a link to our presentation, so you can make an informed decision as to whether this is a right fit for you."

Then I may add, "Because this isn't for everyone. I definitely want you to take a look at this to see if it's a right fit for you."

At this point your prospect is thinking, "I really hope it is!"

CHAPTER 25 - THE FOLLOW UP

If you are sending your prospect some kind of information, and it makes sense to schedule a follow up, this is the process.

Step 1. Schedule The Follow Up ASAP & Be Specific

Pro Tip: Never just send your prospect away without setting up the proper expectations!

We're still asking questions and gaining a commitment from our prospects, even at this point.

They are not allowed to simply go away and get back to us, when they feel like it.

This will decrease your chance of the sale.

You are still setting the agenda, even for the follow up!

Figure out, roughly, how long it takes for a typical prospect to go through the information you are about to send them.

Then to gain their commitment, you're going to ask;

Question: "It's going to take about an hour and a half for you to go through the presentation/information. *How quick do you think you can have this done by?"*

Do not let your prospect decide when you're going to talk again.

You want to try and schedule the follow up as soon as possible after they've watched/ read through the information you've sent them. (Or whatever it is you're directing them to).

Ideally, it needs to be within 24 hours, because you want to keep your prospect within that buying zone. Within the emotional state.

They're excited at this point!

You want them to watch it as soon as possible.

Their answer to this question, will often tell you how serious they are too!

I would suggest encouraging your prospects to go through the information immediately after your consultation.

If you can get your prospect to do this whilst they're excited and everything is fresh in their mind, and you schedule the follow up immediately after that, you're much more likely to get the sale.

You're much more likely to get the sale as they've just been through the process.

If it can't be immediate, try to arrange the follow up within 24 hours.

Again, be super specific, so they know exactly what's happening next.

You're setting the agenda.

You're saying what's happening.

Your prospects will love this because it's organised and it's clear.

Be specific on exactly what they need to do!

Even if it's as specific as 'click this link within the email.'

'Watch this video up until minute X.'

'Open this link, and click here.'

Be very specific.

If you can walk them through the steps as they're doing it, even better!

Tell them exactly when you're scheduling the follow up.

Date and time.

Get them to add it to their calendar.

Increase your chances of the sale!

Recap: Remember at the beginning of this book we said, you want to be comfortable with a yes, and you also want to be totally ok and comfortable with getting a 'no'.

No is an outcome!

No, allows you to move on and stop wasting time.

What you don't want is wishy washy.

What you don't want is a 'maybe.'

"I'll think about it." This is what you want to avoid at all costs.

"I'll think about it," means, you may never hear from me again.

And you're left guessing.

You want to know what's happening next.

It needs to be clear.

You will get so many more sales when things are clear!

Back in my early days of selling, before all my experience and training, I used to let so many people off the hook.

Let people mess me about.

Let people waste my time.

Let people get back to me when they were ready.

And most of the time I'd never hear from them again.

Pro Tip: When I scheduled follow ups within 24 hours of the initial consultation my conversion rate majorly improved! I closed way more sales!

The sooner I scheduled the follow up the more sales I closed.

If your information video is only short, say 10 minutes long. Can you play the video whilst you're on the consultation?

Don't send them away if you can find a way to keep them there.

Question example;

Question: "How quick can you finish watching X by?"

Think about the answer.

This forces your prospect to think how quick they can get through the information, and they're likely to give you a quicker time for the follow up.

I had a lady recently that said, "I can watch it within the next 2 hours as I'm going away on holiday tomorrow. So, it needs to be done today."

She watched the information I sent, and emailed within 2 hours saying, "I want to go for the $2000 option."

Boom. Sale closed.

Now not all sales happen this way, but because she'd just been through the process and everything was fresh in her mind she did it, there and then.

She was ready.

Step 2. Frame The Follow Up

When you send your prospect away to watch or read more information you actually *want* them to watch it!

Remember they're excited at this point.

But if you frame the follow up, you will also increase your chances of your prospect actually watching the information and following through on the follow up.

It looks something like this;

You say. "Okay, so when you watch this presentation, it is going to show you exactly how to (insert what they've just told you they want)."

Be sure to repeat their words to them.

Not your interpretation of the words, their exact words.

Examples;

"Okay, so when you watch this presentation, this is going to show you exactly how you can lose 2 stone in the next 6 months."

"This is going to show you how you can make that additional income so you can leave your job."

"This is going to show you how to earn the extra money you're looking for, so that you can finally go on that holiday with your children, and you can spend more time with them."

Your prospect is much more likely to follow through and watch it, as you've just told them it's going to give them what they want.

Framing The Follow Up Continued

Next you want to frame what is going to happen on the follow up call.

This prepares your prospect with the right expectations *prior* to the follow up.

Adding this into my process made a big difference for me, as it stopped people from saying, "I need to think about it." Or, "Can I let you know?"

"I need to think about it." Often translated, means, "You may never hear from me again…"

And you don't want that.

This is how you frame the follow up;

You say, "On our next call, we'll make a decision as to whether you'd like to join us or get the product (insert the correct outcome)."

Roughly translated, this is saying, 'We're not there to mess around on the next call, we're there to make a decision.

So, you need to go away and do everything you need to do in between now and the next time we speak to make sure you're ready to make a decision.

If that means speaking to your spouse, or taking a look at your finances, we're going to make a decision on the next call."

Obviously you don't say the above. But, in essence this is what you're framing your prospect to go and do.

Be ready to make a decision on the next follow up.

Now, that doesn't mean that every person does, but a heck of a lot more do.

Again, because you're setting the agenda.

Framing The Follow Up - Going One Step Further

Now, you can just leave the framing with the above.

But I highly recommend you go one step further.

The more you can 'frame' what is going to happen on the next call and set your prospect up for the right expectations, so they know exactly what's going to happen, you'll close more sales.

Example;

You. "On the next call we're going to make a decision. Typically, what happens when people turn up to the next call is, they're in 1 of 3 places.

That is, they're either ready to join, and we just get started.

Or, they're ready to join and they need to look at their finances. We help them with that as we have different options available.

Or, they turn up to the next call, and it's not for them.

And I'm completely okay with you being any of those points."

Let's break this down.

By saying this, you're reassuring your prospect that, "Hey it's ok for you to come on the next call and tell me no."

This builds trust and puts your prospect at ease.

But it also acts as a take-away.

Your prospect may think, "Well, I don't want to be a no! I want to be one of the first 2 options."

You are framing the follow up.

The prospect should be thinking, "I've got to turn up to that call and be 1 of the 3 options."

Not a 'maybe'.

Or, 'I'll think about it.'

Frame how you want the follow up to go.

Prospects love this, as it's clear and gives them direction.

CHAPTER 26 - THANK THEM FOR THEIR TIME

Now you have framed the follow up, thank them for their time and finish the call.

(Remember, you may have already closed your prospect at this point, refer to previous chapters).

However, if you are scheduling a follow up, thank your prospect for sharing their information.

You've asked some challenging questions there, and chances are, your prospects have been vulnerable and they've been real with you.

This is the best sale, when it's an authentic one.

So I always say, "I really appreciate your time and appreciate you being so authentic with me. It's been lovely getting to know you and I look forward to speaking to you tomorrow (or whenever it is you've scheduled the follow up)."

CHAPTER 27 - BEING AFRAID OF A 'NO'

I used to be so scared of getting a 'no'.

I wanted to avoid it at all costs.

Until my mentor taught me, "You look at 'no' as a win."

I was like, "How is no a win?"

He replied, "Because no is a positive outcome. No means you can close the chapter and move on."

Think about that for a second.

What you don't want is, "I'll think about it."

That's not a positive outcome. It's not a clear outcome.

It leaves you not knowing what's going to happen next.

It also wastes your time.

We want a 'Yes' obviously, but you need to be comfortable with a 'no'.

No is a win.

No, is a clear outcome.

No, also means you can ask for a *referral.*

You've just spent all this time with your prospect. They really trust you now.

They like you, they know you.

Don't be afraid to say, "I appreciate the time we've spent together. Can I keep in contact with you in case anything changes? Also, do you know someone who this might be a perfect fit for?"

This is your perfect chance to get a warm referral.

It's another reason to be comfortable with a 'no.'

CHAPTER 28 - BEING DESPERATE

Rule of thumb;

When you're desperate, you lose the sale.

When you act as if you don't need it, you actually get it.

Desperation pushes your prospect away.

When you tell your prospect you're comfortable with a no, they usually want it more.

Think of a sales person in a shop. You enter the store, and they come straight over asking if you'd like any help.

Almost with an air of desperation.

I don't know about you, but that instantly puts me off! And I reply, "No thank you, I'm fine."

You have to be comfortable.

Practice and work on your posture.

And you will close more sales.

Chapter 29 - The Money Objection

This is a big one.

And if you've been around in sales for some time, I'm sure you're very aware of it too!

What I want you to know is that for some prospects, the money objection is real.

They genuinely may want what you have to offer, but their finances won't allow it.

For this prospect, it's actually not a loss as you can look at ways to help them.

Perhaps you have some kind of payment plan scheme?

Perhaps you have an alternative product?

An alternative plan?

Your prospect wants what you have, so it's simply a case of working with them to find something that fits.

However, for a lot of prospects the money objection is a cop out.

(I will share a question with you shortly that will help you determine whether the money objection is real or not).

Now, I don't want you to start viewing your prospects as liars. *I just want you to see that many, many prospects will say they don't have the money, when in fact it has nothing to do with the money.*

Just think about it. If someone wants something, generally they'll do whatever it takes to get it.

Read that line again.

Think of the amount of people you know that own things they can't afford.

Cars, mobile phones, anything!

If someone wants something, they'll get it.

Or they'll find a way to get it.

So how do you figure out if the money objection is real?

You simply ask;

"Ok, I hear that you're saying that you don't have the money. Let me ask, if you did have the finances would you still want to join?"

Or, "If you did have the finances would you still want to buy X?"

If your prospect doesn't respond with an immediate definite 'YES!', then typically money isn't the issue.

There's usually another reason why they're not buying.

If your prospect pauses.

Or they reply with an, "Ermmm."

Or, "I'm not sure?"

This is a clear sign that it's not the money.

They're withholding the true reason.

Something else is holding them back, and you need to ask more questions to try and see what's going on.

One of the easiest questions you can ask in response to this is;

"Tell me more about that."

This will usually allow you to uncover what is going on, and guide you to answering their concern.

Chapter 30 - The Spouse Objection

If your prospect is hinting that they will need to speak to their spouse before making a decision, first know that this is very common.

Now, this will also, usually be determined by the price point of whatever it is you're selling.

If it's higher, this is typically when this objection occurs.

If they give you a hint of this on your first call, you can handle this objection here at this point, and stop it from becoming an objection on the follow up call.

So, instead of getting to the follow up, and they say exactly the same thing again, "I still need to speak with my spouse," and you knew this on the previous call. A really powerful question that you can say is;

"Okay, great. So, typically, how does your spouse respond when you approach them about things like this?"

And you get them to role play and think through this situation, *before* it's even happened.

This is really powerful.

Let's role play;

You. "Typically, how would your husband respond when you go to him over something like this?"

Prospect. "Well, he's usually quite supportive."

You. "That's good. So, what do you feel needs to happen when you have the conversation? What needs to happen between now and the next call so you are ready to make a decision either way?"

You're basically getting your prospect to map out what they need to do in order to make a decision.

You're overcoming the objection before it's even happened in a sense.

And you're saving yourself time that perhaps may have been wasted.

Now, you may be thinking (as I did when i first got taught this strategy), this is a tad uncomfortable.

To be talking to your prospect about how they're going to speak to their spouse.

Try it on.

Give it a try and you may be surprised like I was!

What I found was prospects really enjoyed talking to someone about this issue.

And it allowed me to help my prospects.

I was able to help them think about that discussion before it occurred.

Almost like creating a plan of action for the conversation.

Even just helping your prospect to think about how the conversation is going to pan out, before they have it, can really help them.

CHAPTER 31 - SABOTAGING THE SALE.

What I'm about to say next, is really important.

Are you someone who sabotages the sale?

<u>If your prospect is ready to buy. Close them.</u>

Don't sabotage the sale.

If your prospect is giving you signs that they just want to buy, *don't get in the way of the sale.*

Let me explain.

Have you ever found that when your prospect is ready to buy, you continue talking?

As if you're still trying to convince them this is right for them?

I used to do it.

My prospect would give me all the signs they'd want to buy, even at times saying

'Yes I'd like to join.' And instead of shutting up and closing them, I'd keep talking.

I'd get in the way of the sale.

If you are someone who is nervous about making the sale, or you have money issues. Perhaps some money blocks that you're unaware of. Your mindset may be off when it comes to selling.

You may be doing this without realising.

Do you find you get nervous when you close the sale?

Be careful you're not sabotaging the sale by continuing to talk and convince, when they've said yes!

You simply, stop talking and process the sale!

As soon as someone says, "I'm ready to buy."

You say. "Great! Let's get you started."

That's it.

Don't try and then reconfirm to them that they're making the right decision!

Just close the sale.

- FINAL WORDS

There you have it…

A step-by-step process to closing more sales.

You may need to read this book a few times and I highly recommend you give the questions a try, at least once!

Try them on for size.

See which ones fit.

See which ones you prefer to ask.

I hope you've found this book helpful and it's given you more insight and tools into becoming a master closer.

Throughout this process you haven't tried to convince your prospect once.

The beauty is, it's your prospect, every step of the way, convincing themselves.

You're simply holding their hand and guiding them.

You just need to ask the right questions, take them by the hand, and help them cross the finish line.

I hope you've had some revelations, increased your knowledge and you're ready to put this into practice!

I wish you all the best in your endeavors to close more sales.

To your success!

Emma

****

Special Masterclass

THE SELLING PLAN:

Over 4 x hours of recorded training from Emma.

Would you love access to a pre-recorded Live webinar that Emma held covering the Selling Plan in detail? Including a special 2 *x hour bonus training on overcoming objections?*

Get access to Emma's training:

The Proven Step-By-Step Selling Plan To Close More Clients & Make More Sales

Including special bonus 2 x hour training on Overcoming Objections

Get All The Details Here:

The Selling Plan Special Masterclass

pagecreatorpro.com/nuyouuk/the-selling-plan/

May I ask you a small favor?

If you enjoyed this book, would you be so kind to leave me a review?

Reviews on Amazon are incredibly helpful-both for other readers to decide whether this book will be useful to them and for authors like myself to get the word out. Your support is much appreciated!

Thank you for taking the time.

To your success!

Emma

Get Your Copy Now:

FREE COURSE

Do you need more leads for your business?

Need more clients?

Would you like to know how to ATTRACT leads to you online, 24/7, using social media, without having to chase or bug family and friends?

Get Access To My Free Course Here

FINALLY!

A Better Way To Attract & Recruit People On Social Media- Without Having To Chase Family and Friends

ABOUT THE AUTHOR

Emma Jones, founder of *Success With Emma Jones.com* is an online entrepreneur specialising in marketing and social media.

Having been successful in multiple business ventures online, Emma now helps other budding entrepreneurs to create thriving businesses online.

Emma loves everything to do with online marketing and advertising and loves to teach it to her students too. Her online training programmes and courses have helped thousands around the world get more savvy online and more importantly, get results.

A born entrepreneur she loves nothing more than helping other entrepreneurial minded individuals realise their greatness and fulfill it.

Emma's clients and students often say she allows them to believe in themselves and achieve their full potential.

Emma helps them to create success online and build the lifestyle of their dreams.

When Emma's not writing, coaching, going Live on Social Media or delivering one of her training programs - you can find her spending quality time with her family, dancing (a lifelong hobby of hers), watching reruns of friends or generally running around after her kids!

You can find Emma here;

Website:
www.SuccessWithEmmaJones.com

Facebook:
https://www.facebook.com/SuccessWithEmmaJones/

Instagram:
https://www.instagram.com/successwithemmajones/

Disclaimer

My vision is to help you with the skills necessary to close more sales. As stipulated by law, I cannot and do not make any guarantees about your ability to get results or earn any money with the skills, information, ideas and processes mentioned in this book. Your results are completely up to you, your level of awareness, expertise, the action you take and the service you provide to others. Any testimonials, financial numbers mentioned in this book or on any of our web pages should not be considered as a promise of potential earnings.

Printed in Great Britain
by Amazon

83035434R00099